F^{OR SEVERAL DI} slept while thei been threatened, chipped away, and eroded by a series of innocuous-sounding and nearly imperceptible decisions. Building on years of writing, conference-going, resolution-passing, and networking, opponents of unfettered U.S. sovereignty have been fashioning constraints on the exercise of our fundamental demo-cratic rights, national power, and legitimacy. We have been locked in a struggle between sovereignty and "global governance" that most Americans didn't even know was hap-pening. Not surprisingly, therefore, the "Amer-icanists" have been losing to the "globalists," and the general public does not yet appreciate the chasm between these two worldviews. In fact, there hasn't been much of a battle else-where in the world either; we can have a truly robust debate only in America because of the basic faith we have in our own institutions and freedoms.

The important point is to get the discus-sion started. It is time for a fire bell in the night,

We can have a truly robust debate only in America because of the basic faith we have in our own institutions and freedoms.

a little contemporary common sense about what has been going on all around us. This is not a confrontation over that favorite buzzword, "globalization," and its implications for commerce, culture, and travel, but a debate about power and government – *our* power and *our* government.

KEY ISSUES IN THE SOVEREIGNTY DEBATE DURING THE OBAMA ERA

What Is "Sovereignty," and Why Is It Especially Important for the United States?

Sovereignty may seem like an enormous abstraction, gauzy and hard to understand.

Indeed, it has a huge range of definitions, complicated and often contradictory, thus ironically making it easier for some people to believe that sovereignty is less important than it actually is. Coined originally in Europe to describe the authority of kings and queens – the "sovereigns" – the concept evolved rapidly after the 1648 Peace of Westphalia to refer to nation-states. National sovereignty now generally encompasses the fullest range of state power: dealing with other international actors (foreign and defense policy); control over borders (immigration and customs); and exercising authority domestically (economic and social policy). Whatever the intricacies and complexities of measuring and exercising legitimate governmental authority, these powers are basic.

Despite the raging academic debates over the precise definition and measurement of sovereignty, for Americans, the idea is actually quite straightforward. The Founding Fathers understood it implicitly, and they took care in the Declaration of Independence to explain why they were ready "to assume among the powers of the earth, the separate and equal station to which the laws of nature and of nature's God entitle them." On July 4, 1776, our sovereignty moved from George III to us, "We the People of the United States," as the Constitution later described it.

This is fundamental. For Americans, sovereignty is not simply an academic abstraction. For us, sovereignty is our control over our own government. Thus, advocates of "sharing" or "pooling" U.S. sovereignty with international organizations to address "global" problems are really saying we should cede some of our sovereignty to institutions that other nations will also influence or even control. That is unquestionably a formula for reducing U.S. autonomy and reducing our control over government. Since most Americans believe they do not have adequate control over the federal government *now*, it is no wonder they are reluctant to cede even more of that control to distant bodies where our influence is reduced or uncertain. Indeed, wasn't that what our Revolution was about in the first place?

What Is "Global Governance," and Why Is It a Threat to U.S. Sovereignty?

Opponents of U.S. sovereignty used to applaud "world government," thus providing an easy target, since there has never been more than a shred of sympathy here for such an idea. Over time, academics and activists alike have therefore adopted the phrase "global governance" to describe a more piecemeal, less rhetorically threatening approach, reflecting also that not all global governance advocates themselves feel comfortable that their final objective is world government. The soothingly entitled 1995 blueprint, *Our Global Neighborhood*, argues that global governance "is part of the evolution of human efforts to organize life on the planet, and the process will always be going on." This underlines the debates between Americanists, who want to preserve our sovereignty, and globalists, who want to see it, in whole or part, constrained or transferred to international organizations.

Most Americans, busy with their daily lives, have paid scant attention to the global governance debate in places like the United Nations, the European Union, and the universities. Nonetheless, academics and the international Left, despite their differences, can be heard repeating endlessly, like a Greek chorus, that national sovereignty is diminishing inexorably because of the press of global problems. They emphasize the EU example, where the drift of national authority toward EU headquarters in Brussels and away from London, Berlin, and other capitals has indeed seemed inevitable and irreversible. Global governance advocates frequently minimize the importance of reduced sovereignty, citing, for example, the treaty-making authority. Although normally understood as an elemental example of exercising national sovereignty, treaties, say the globalists, actually limit sovereignty by reducing the scope for unilateral action. Since treaties have been around from time immemorial, what is the problem today with more ambitious treaties that diminish sovereignty somewhat more visibly? Isn't the whole argument just one of degree rather than basic philosophy? Why be so uncomfortable?

This verbal and conceptual bait and switch has, for its proponents, the further advantage of obscuring what is happening at any particular point in the seemingly endless process of negotiation that facilitates diminutions in U.S. sovereignty. Unquestionably, most threats to sovereignty grow like a coral reef rather than manifesting themselves in a particular crisis or a made-for-TV decisive moment. Moreover, the debate over sovereignty and global governance is diffuse and opaque because the battlefront stretches over a vast territory, and the scope of activity along that front varies dramatically.

The field of combat is neither well-understood nor well-watched by politicians or the media. There is nothing mysterious or sinister about the process of international negotiations, including those with profound sovereignty implications. Indeed, it is precisely the ordinariness and depressingly unremarkable nature and pace of such negotiations that guarantee they do not cause red flags to pop up until each negotiation is essentially complete and the final agreement available for public and legislative review. Even then, the final texts are likely to be obscure, technical, and jargon-filled.

The key lies in seeing the big picture. In fact, global governance advocates have crossed a clear line of demarcation. The millennia-old notion of treaties, whether political, military, or economic, expanded after World War II into a completely different realm, a conceptual breakout distinguishing what has been afoot for the past half-century from the historical treaty process. The EU led the way with its regional experiment, and EU diplomats and their worldwide allies sympathetic to their transnational aspirations have been spreading the gospel.

So common and well-accepted is this approach in Europe that its leaders now disdain to hide their objectives, in effect aspiring to do worldwide to national sovereignty what they have so successfully done in Europe. Fittingly and revealingly, the EU's first president, former Belgian Prime Minister Herman Van Rompuy, upon taking office on November 19, 2009, called 2009 "the first year of global governance, with the establishment of the G-20 in the middle of the financial crisis. The climate conference in Copenhagen is another step toward the global management of our planet." Advocates of global governance in the United States are not yet so outspoken in general public discourse, but they believe exactly the same things and say so in their obscure academic journals and debates. They have long been hard at work on this issue, and they almost uniformly supported Barack Obama for president in 2008.

What Is President Obama's View on U.S. Sovereignty?

Barack Obama is our first post-American president – someone who sees his role in foreign policy less as an advocate for America's "parochial" interests and more as a "citizen of the world," in his own phrase. He broadly embodies many European social democratic values, including those regarding sovereignty, so it was not surprising that an ecstatic student said after hearing him on one of his first overseas trips, "He sounds like a European." Indeed he does.

Barack Obama is our first post-American president — someone who sees his role in foreign policy less as an advocate for America's "parochial" interests and more as a "citizen of the world," in his own phrase.

Understanding Obama's view of America's proper role in the world and how it relates to other nations is critical. Strikingly, he neither cares very much about national security issues, nor has he had much relevant professional experience. During the 2008 campaign, he repeatedly contended that the world was not very threatening to U.S. interests, and in his first year in office, other than the usual processionals abroad, he has spent as little time as possible on international issues. His preoccupation with radically restructuring our domestic economy is obvious.

Obama's worldview is almost exclusively Wilsonian, as his public statements reveal. In his September 2009 address to the U.N. General Assembly, for example, Obama said:

> [I]t is my deeply held belief that in the year 2009 – more than at any point in human history – the interests of nations and peoples are shared. . . . In an era when our destiny is shared, power is no longer a zero-sum game. No one nation can or should try to dominate another nation. No world order that elevates one nation or group of people over another will succeed. No balance of power among nations will hold.

In 1916, Woodrow Wilson said, "There must be, not a balance of power, but a community of power; not organized rivalries, but an organized common peace" resting on "the moral force of the public opinion of the world." Removing the dates in these remarks makes it nearly impossible to differentiate Wilson from Obama.

Thus, while Obama's naive multilateralism is not unprecedented in U.S. history, his disregard of the 90 years of global conflagration, carnage, and catastrophe since Wilson is both breathtaking and unnerving. It reflects, moreover, the obsession with process rather than substance that permeates Obama's broader international perspective; for example, his belief that negotiation is actually a policy rather than merely a technique.

Critically, however, Obama's worldview extends well beyond Wilsonian multilateralism. Asked by a reporter about American exceptionalism, Obama replied, "I believe in American exceptionalism, just as I suspect that the Brits believe in British exceptionalism and the Greeks believe in Greek exceptionalism." There are 192 members of the U.N., and Obama could have gone on to mention "Peruvian exceptionalism," "Nigerian exceptionalism," and "Papua New Guinean exceptionalism." Obviously, if everyone is exceptional, no one is.

U.S. exceptionalism comes in many varieties, but they share the core notion that our founding and history give America a special place in the world. John Winthrop, governor of the Massachusetts Bay Colony, paraphrased scripture and said, "We must consider that we shall be as a city upon a hill," which Ronald Reagan edited slightly to describe us as "a shining city on a hill." Others call us "the New Jerusalem," but it was the perceptive Frenchman Alexis de Tocqueville who first wrote, in *Democracy in America*, that "[t]he position of the Americans is therefore quite exceptional, and it may be believed that no democratic people will ever be placed in a similar one."

Obama's remoteness from American exceptionalism has been revealingly noted by his enthusiasts as well as his critics. Following Obama's speech on D-day's 65th anniversary, for example, Evan Thomas of *Newsweek* hailed Obama as a marked contrast to Ronald Reagan, who spoke at the 40th anniversary.

> *Well, we were the good guys in 1984, it felt that way. It hasn't felt that way in recent years. So Obama's had, really, a different task. . . . [R]eagan was all about America. . . . Obama is "we are above that now." We are not just parochial, we're not just chauvinistic, we're not just provincial. We stand for something. I mean in a way Obama's standing above the country, above — above the world, he's sort of God. He's going to bring all different sides together.*

One can imagine Obama saying nearly the same thing about himself.

Obama is the first person holding such views to be elected president, but he merely reflects what has long been the dominant opinion within the Democratic Party's top leadership. John Kerry in the 2004 campaign argued that U.S. foreign policy has to pass a "global test" of legitimacy, essentially meaning approval by the U.N. Security Council. In his 1988 acceptance speech at the Republican convention, then-Vice President George H. W. Bush captured the contrast between himself and his opponent, Massachusetts Gov. Michael Dukakis, tellingly: "He sees America as another pleasant country on the U.N. roll call, somewhere between Albania and Zimbabwe. And I see America as the leader – a unique nation with a special role in the world."

Bush's 1988 description of Dukakis easily fits Obama today, as his repeated implicit denigration of a special role for America shows ("No world order that elevates one nation or group of people over another will succeed"). With Obama predilections in mind, let us turn to the pending issues where Obama's decisions and policies can decisively affect U.S. sovereignty.

* * *

Threats to U.S. sovereignty are both imminent and long-term. They do not all share common characteristics, nor are they necessarily immediately obvious as threats. One element that runs through many of them, however, is the concept of international "norming" – the idea that America should base its policies on the international consensus, rather than making its own decisions as a constitutional democracy. Using norming, the international Left seeks to constrain U.S. sovereignty by moving our domestic political debate to align with broader international opinion. Because of the centrality of individual freedom in the United States, norming advocates are invariably on the left of the political spectrum; there are simply no other nations out there are as liberty-oriented as we are.

One way to drive norming is through votes in multilateral organizations like the

192-member United Nations. Operating under the "one nation, one vote" principle, the General Assembly routinely passes resolutions where the United States finds itself not only in opposition, but often with only a handful of others voting with it. "One nation, one vote" has a surface democratic ring to it, but it is in fact profoundly antidemocratic and certainly affords no legitimacy to what happens on the General Assembly floor. While being "isolated" in international bodies may be uncomfortable, a point the international Left stresses

If American exceptionalism means only that it took us longer and a different route to get to European social democracy, the whole enterprise would hardly have been worth it.

to embarrass us, it often may be the only way to protect our sovereignty and our interests. After all, if American exceptionalism means only that it took us longer and a different route to get to European social democracy, the whole enterprise would hardly have been worth it.

Let us turn now to several critical areas where U.S. sovereignty is under siege.

American National Security

Strong defenses are critical to national survival, so it is hardly surprising that opponents of unfettered U.S. sovereignty strive endlessly to constrain our ability to act in self-defense. Limiting or transferring decisional authority on security issues to international bodies is thus a core divide between Americanists and globalists.

Nowhere is this issue more graphically framed than in debates over the legitimacy of the use of force. In 1999, during NATO's air campaign against Yugoslavia — which the U.N. Security Council had not authorized because of a threatened Russian veto — Secretary-General Kofi Annan complained that "[u]nless the Security Council is restored to its preeminent position as the sole source of legitimacy on the use of force, we are on a dangerous path to anarchy." Shortly thereafter, Annan said that military action taken without council approval constituted a threat to the "very core of the international security system. . . . Only the [U.N.] Charter provides a universally accepted legal basis for the use of force."

This, of course, is conceptually identical to Kerry's argument for a "global test" for U.S. foreign policy, namely, that someone else must approve it before it can be considered legitimate. Interestingly, shortly after Annan's comments, then-Delaware Sen. Joe Biden said, "Nobody in the Senate agrees with that. Nobody in the Senate agrees with that. There is nothing to debate. He is dead, flat, unequivocally wrong. . . . It is a statement that an overexuberant politician like I am might make on another matter, but I hope he did not mean it, if he did. I love him, but he is flat-out wrong." We will now see, of course, whether Vice President Biden's opinion remains the same under President Obama.

A dramatic contrast to the global-test approach to foreign policy, which still involves effective multilateral activity, is the U.S.-led Proliferation Security Initiative (PSI). PSI now has more than 90 participating countries working to stop the international trafficking of weapons and materials of mass destruction. PSI has no secretary-general, no bureaucracy, no headquarters, no endless diplomatic meetings. It simply focuses, often clandestinely, on working to prevent or interdict shipments of contraband material. As one British diplomat put it, "PSI is an activity, not an organization." In fact, PSI is precisely the kind of multilateral activity that protects our national security while respecting our sovereignty, and thus disproves the charges of those who complain that U.S. sovereignty advocates favor only unilateral action and therefore lack "legitimacy."

These contrasting approaches highlight the options facing President Obama. Moreover, many national security issues, particularly those involving use of force, merge quickly into the appropriate role of "international law." While respected scholars disagree strongly on the force and scope of international law, those urging its expansion most emphatically are also those most at odds with the continuing vitality of American sovereignty. Thus, while many in the mainstream of American politics debate the utility, wisdom, and implications of international law policies, we can focus on the sharp edges, where international law advocates are trying to tie Gulliver down in ways most Americans find utterly unacceptable.

Law, "International Law," and American Sovereignty

To President Obama, the concept of international law is palpable, as his September 2009 speech to the U.N. Security Council emphasized: "[W]e must demonstrate that international law is not an empty promise, and that treaties will be enforced." Many in his administration are doing their utmost to subvert America's well-deserved reputation as an adherent of the rule of law by subordinating it to the dangerous concept that international law, as defined by its high priests, overrides our domestic law, including in the judiciary. Actually, what is or is not legally binding about international law, particularly customary international law, is wide open to dispute. Customary international law used to refer to "state practice" in international affairs, a generally sensible way of deciding such questions as navigation protocols, reflecting what seafaring states have done over the centuries. In recent decades, however, the academic Left has seized on customary law as a fertile field for imposing its own ideological standards internationally and binding countries to "laws" they never explicitly approved.

Because democratic debates in constitutional systems like ours are so unsatisfying and often so unproductive for America's statists, they have, in essence, launched an international power play to move outside of our legal systems. They find much greater prospects for success in international forums like the United Nations than in the U.S. Congress. Hence, the role and limits of international law, determining what is legally binding for our international conduct and domestic policy, will be a critical area of debate in the coming years.

The most visible, immediate impact of President Obama's fascination with international law appears in the global war against terrorism, a term he tries to avoid. Instead, he adopted the view widely held in Europe and among legal theorists that terrorist threats and attacks should be treated under the criminal law enforcement paradigm, rather than as attacks on America subject to the law of war. The question is whether we treat terrorists simply as bank robbers on steroids or as national security threats to which we should respond in legitimate self-defense. The Obama administration strongly supports the criminal law paradigm, which most Americans emphatically reject.

Thus, reflecting the law-enforcement approach, Obama rapidly ordered the closure of the Guantanamo Bay terrorist detention facility and either the release of those still detained or their transfer to the United States. He also pushed to abandon "enhanced interrogation" techniques and insisted upon trying as many terrorists as possible in civilian courts, under ordinary criminal law procedures rather than in military tribunals. This mindset's strong ideological roots reflect the administration's fundamental acceptance of leftist conventional wisdom on international law. Under this view, for Obama, closing Gitmo is not just good policy but, more importantly, "norms" America with international opinion on handling terrorists.

Why we should defer to international norms on terrorism is, to say the least, unclear. The U.N. has repeatedly tried and failed to reach a comprehensive definition of terrorism. Its continuing inability to agree on something so fundamental helps explain why the U.N., particularly the Security Council, has been AWOL in the war on terrorism, and why international norms should not dissuade us even slightly from legitimate self-defense efforts.

Unfortunately, mishandling the war against terrorism doesn't end with distorting the correct legal and political paradigms to combat it. The Obama administration has broader ambitions as well, including an ill-concealed desire to join the International Criminal Court (ICC). Although billed as a successor to the Nuremberg tribunals, the ICC, in fact, amounts to a giant opportunity to second-guess the United States and the actions we take in self-defense. The ICC's enormous potential prosecutorial power awaits only the opportunity to expand almost without limit. The Clinton administration initially signed the ICC's founding document, the Rome Statute, in June 1998, but there was no prospect that the Senate would ratify it. The Bush administration unsigned the treaty and entered into more than 100 bilateral agreements with countries to prevent our citizens from being delivered into the ICC's custody. To date, the ICC has proceeded slowly, partly in the hope of enticing the United States to cooperate with it, and the Bush administration succumbed to it in its final years. The ICC's friends under President Obama want to go even further. Secretary of State Hillary Clinton said in 2009, for example, that it was "a great regret but it is a fact we are not yet a signatory" to the Rome Statute, signaling unmistakably what she hopes to do.

The Obama administration's willingness to submit U.S. conduct to international judicial review also extends to the concept of "universal jurisdiction," which permits even countries utterly unrelated to an event to initiate criminal prosecutions regarding it. The administration has yet to say, for example, that it will oppose potential European efforts to prosecute those responsible for enhanced interrogation techniques. This devotion to international norms is designed to intimidate U.S. decision makers, military forces, and intelligence agents, and violates basic democratic precepts that we are responsible for and fully capable of holding our government to its responsibilities under our Constitution.

In fact, limiting America's military options and capabilities through international agreements and organizations is a high priority for the Obama administration. It has been hard at work since Inauguration Day negotiating with Russia to significantly reduce both America's nuclear weapons and delivery systems. The administration appears open to imposing new constraints on our missile defense programs. These were previously eliminated in 2001 by the Bush administration's withdrawal from the 1972 Anti-Ballistic Missile Treaty, which barred us from building national missile defenses. President Obama has already abandoned missile defense sites in Poland and the Czech Republic that were intended to protect the continental United States. Any missile defense budget cuts will cause enormous damage, no matter what is ultimately agreed with Moscow.

Moreover, the president's aspiration, articulated in his 2009 Prague speech, to achieve a world without nuclear weapons is well on track, whether or not other nuclear nations (and proliferators) follow suit. Obama has committed to a multitude of multilateral arms-control treaties and negotiations, such as again pressing for Senate ratification of the Comprehensive Nuclear Test Ban Treaty (previously defeated by a Senate vote of 51–48 on October 13, 1999). Undoubtedly, the Landmines Convention, another Clinton administration legacy (adopted in Ottawa in December 1997) will also reappear on the administration's agenda. In addition, the president wants to negotiate treaties to stop new production of fissile material, to prevent an outer space "arms race," and to regulate trade in conventional weapons that will have potentially enormous implications for our domestic debate over the Second Amendment and firearms control.

In addition, many senior administration officials have demonstrated their sympathy for using international "human rights" norms on the conduct of war to constrain the United States. Of course, no one advocates uncivilized or inhumane behavior, but the critical point is who defines such behavior and who holds those who violate the accepted standards accountable. Under our Constitution, we are fully capable of deciding how and when to use military force, how our warriors should conduct themselves, and how to deal with those who violate our standards. We do not need international human rights experts, prosecutors, or courts to satisfy our own high standards for American behavior.

This is not the view, however, of those who want to constrain our sovereignty. After all, if we decided what is right and wrong, they couldn't second-guess us and bend us to their views. Having failed to win this point within our political system, however, they simply retreat into international organizations, hoping they and their international leftist allies can win there what they failed to win at home.

Israel is often a preferred target because it is small and even less popular in the elite circles of international law and norming than

---

We do not need international human rights experts, prosecutors, or courts to satisfy our own high standards for American behavior.

---

the United States. Thus, the U.N.'s recent Goldstone report on Israel's 2008–2009 Operation Cast Lead against Hamas in the Gaza Strip (criticized Israel for violations of the law of war, such as the "disproportionate use of force," in ways that severely undermine Israel's inherent right of self-defense.) If such conclusions become widely accepted, they will obviously have direct and substantial effects on our ability to undertake our own self-defense, which is, of course, exactly what the globalists have in mind. The U.N. Human Rights Council,

established in 2006, has proven to be even
worse than its completely discredited prede-
cessor, spending most of its time examining
Israel's defects rather than the world's worst
human-rights violators. Nonetheless, based
on its post-American ideology, the Obama
administration rejoined the council. Unsur-
prisingly, U.S. membership has had no effect
on council decisions, but our return has given
it a legitimacy utterly lacking in our absence.

President Obama has used military force
to protect America, but almost apologetically
and with undisguised longing to do exactly
the opposite. Thus, even when announcing a
substantial increase in U.S. forces in Afghanistan to combat the Taliban, he avowed simul-
taneously his hope to begin withdrawing
those forces in mid-2011. Such a clear signal
of weakness only encourages the Taliban and
al Qaeda to hold on until that point, when
Obama could begin bringing troops home,
perhaps even proclaiming "mission accom-
plished." Ironically, of course, the campaigns
in Afghanistan and Pakistan employ armed

drone aircraft to target and kill terrorist leaders and supporters, although, needless to say, the targets don't get *Miranda* rights read to them. The administration seems unwilling to reconcile these strikes with how it handles terrorists captured in the United States. Already, there are international complaints that the drone attacks are precisely the kinds of "targeted" or "extra-judicial" killings complained about for years when undertaken by Israel. But what conclusion will terrorists draw if they realize that, as with the Christmas Day 2009 bomber, you are likely to be safer if you attack the United States in its homeland rather than in the "Af-Pak" mountains? President Obama should adjust his antiterrorism policy in America to reflect the war paradigm in central Asia.

Economic and Environmental Policy
Threats to Sovereignty

One popular global initiative arising in a variety of contexts and formats is to give global organizations taxing power independent of national governments. First proposed by Yale's James Tobin to tax currency transactions to reduce speculation, the idea of international taxes has expanded to such diverse sources of revenue as bank transfers, international airplane tickets, and royalties from subsea mining. Proceeds from the taxes could be used to finance U.N. agencies, for global warming programs, or for anything else creative minds can conjure.

Central to these proposals is funding international activities without any need for action by national governments, and this stems from frustrations with the United States. Congress has, over the years, frequently withheld "assessed" contributions from the U.N., and critics claimed we were thereby violating our obligations under the U.N. Charter. That claim itself is highly debatable, but there is no question that withholding funds shocked and awed the international bureaucracies. Accordingly, the search was on for ways to end-run Congress and obtain revenue sources that the

What conclusion will terrorists draw if they realize that, as with the Christmas Day 2009 bomber, you are likely to be safer if you attack the United States in its homeland rather than in the "Af-Pak" mountains?

people's representatives could not turn on and off at will.

The issue of international taxing authority will be increasingly prominent and is an issue even in long-pending treaties that President Obama is pressing to ratify, such as the Law of the Sea Treaty (LOST). "Royalties" from undersea mining activities to fund the international authority created under LOST should be understood as one of the treaty's key defects and a dangerous precedent for future "self-funding" international regulatory schemes.

Unquestionably, the mother of all such plans is in the environmental area: the Kyoto/Copenhagen global warming enterprise. Buried in the failed Copenhagen negotiations were critical provisions to generate funding for "climate change" activities completely free of congressional action. There are many grounds to oppose Copenhagen's statist agenda, but the issue of taxation should be one of the most important. Whatever the reality of the earth's changing temperature and humanity's role in it, the fundamental debate should be over the proposed solutions. If increased taxation, regulation, and control at the national or international levels are the answers, we are clearly asking the wrong questions.

Mirroring the threat of the ICC and "universal jurisdiction" in national security, many proposed international economic regulatory schemes also contain tribunals with unchecked judicial or prosecutorial powers. This increased delegation of national authority into essentially unaccountable international tribunals translates as transferring more and more of our own governance beyond our effective constitutional control – and more erosion of U.S. sovereignty.

Sovereignty and Social Issues

The globalists have been extremely active in what we normally consider domestic social issues. Their tactical rationale is clear. Frustrated by not achieving their objectives in domestic U.S. politics, they take their issues international. There, in multilateral negotiations, they typically find far more sympathy for their objectives and policies than in Washington. Encouraged by this welcoming environment, the globalists, often working through nongovernmental organizations (NGOs), negotiate agreements embodying their own policy preferences. They then bring them back to America, often embedded in larger treaty documents that contain unrelated or at least innocuous provisions. By using this back door, the globalists hope to achieve indirectly what they cannot obtain more openly. Moreover, NGOs often participate in international negotiations almost as nation-states, giving the "civil society" activists a second bite at the apple to reach their policy objectives. Most Americans think the debate is over once an issue is resolved in our domestic politics. The globalist NGOs know better.

It is certainly true, and vitally important for protecting our sovereignty, that treaties require a two-thirds Senate vote for ratification, thus leading some to conclude that the backdoor approach is actually more difficult than conventional legislation, which requires only a majority in the House and Senate. Of course, through the increasingly popular vehicle of "legislative-executive agreements," large numbers of measures have been enacted into law by the House and Senate, including trade and tariff agreements and U.S. membership in the World Bank and the International Monetary Fund. The broader point is not process but legislative scrutiny. International agreements are essentially "take it or leave it" propositions, rarely amended during congressional debate. In addition, the domestic effects of many treaty provisions are far from obvious, often intentionally so, and therefore, they do not receive adequate scrutiny. Moreover, many international conventions are adopted routinely and without much thought by other countries, leaving the United States, often one of the few nations not to immediately ratify, exposed to the complaint that we are isolated in the world, usually in the company of undesirables like Sudan and Burma. "What is wrong with the United States?" the treaty advocates lament. The efficacy of this form of political pressure cannot be discounted, although most often what is wrong with the United States is that we actually take treaties seriously, unlike many other countries that ratify them indiscriminately with little or no intention of abiding by them or even paying them much attention.

Take, for example, the issue of gun control, where many proponents are frustrated with their lack of popular domestic support. Beginning in the Clinton administration, pro-gun-control NGOs decided to go international under the guise of curbing international trafficking in "small arms and light weapons." While there is much to be said for responsible protections in arms exports, which United States law has long included, more strictly, in fact, than any other country, the NGOs' real objective was the international limitation on private ownership of firearms.

In 2002, the Bush administration essentially put a stop to those efforts in the U.N. system, a bar that lasted until Obama's inauguration. Now, Secretary of State Clinton is pushing hard for an Arms Trade Treaty that could do what the gun-control advocates have long been seeking. Ellen Tauscher, under-secretary of state for arms control and international security, said in February 2009 that the ongoing negotiations "have broadened so that we now have an A-to-Z list of meetings and forums on how to limit or eliminate small arms, anti-personnel land mines and other indiscriminate weapons." Note how, in her view, guns and rifles for hunting or self-protection are now "indiscriminate weapons" like land mines. Her formulation is a classic example of how advocates can obfuscate their real objectives, and how they operate under the radar screen in domestic American politics until the international treaty is negotiated and brought back to Washington. Then, we are told, we must ratify it or be "isolated" in the world.

This approach has been used over the years against the death penalty. In the United States, at the national and state levels, we have a vigorous democratic debate over the death penalty, sometimes expanding it and sometimes contracting it. In every case, though, we do it after free and open debate. That, however, is not good enough for death-penalty opponents, who can't get what they want in the United States. They too have gone international, using the U.N.'s "human rights" bodies to repeatedly condemn the death penalty. In effect, death-penalty opponents are trying to mobilize international public opinion against the prevailing majority view within the United States, as well as trying in U.S. courts to use unrelated treaties to prevent the penalty from being applied. This often surprises people from democracies. During his first months in office in 2007, for example, U.N. Secretary-General Ban Ki-moon remarked that the issue of the death penalty was each nation's to decide on its own, reflecting his understanding as a citizen of South Korea, which still has the death penalty. Ban was all but tarred and feathered in U.N. circles for not recognizing the long string of U.N. resolutions opposing the death penalty. In America, citizens might well have asked, "What business is it of the U.N. even to have votes on the legitimacy of the death penalty?"

The same internationalization of domestic issues appears in a host of other social issues: abortion; family law and the relationships between parent and child (the Convention on the Rights of the Child); and discrimination based on gender (the Convention on the Elimination of All Forms of Discrimination Against Women), race (the U.N. Committee on the Elimination of Racial Discrimination), or disability (Convention on the Rights of Persons

With Disabilities). The issue here is not, for example, appropriate protections against discrimination, but who should decide such questions. Should it be American citizens operating under our Constitution or international agreements with nations that care little about fundamental freedoms or the importance of democratic debate? This is where the rubber truly meets the road on sovereignty.

PROTECTING AMERICAN SOVEREIGNTY IN THE AGE OF OBAMA

We must take threats to American sovereignty and efforts to expand the scope of global governance seriously. Failure to do so, and its inevitable consequences, will only be our fault. As James Madison said in 1788 during the debate over ratifying the Constitution: "[T]here are more instances of the abridgment of the freedom of the people by gradual and silent encroachments of those in power than by violent and sudden usurpations. . . ."

So what must we do during the remainder

of the Obama presidency, given the enormous authority for international affairs vested in the executive branch and his current considerable majorities in both houses of Congress? While the answer is discouraging, it should remind us yet again why elections matter.

First, and most importantly, we must understand better how and where sovereignty issues arise. Too often, even in areas directly affecting national security, we do not appreciate the issues at stake. Important threats to sovereignty may arise more often on what we consider domestic policies. All of us, therefore, need to be alert to the implications of policy issues for U.S. sovereignty. You can be sure the globalists are. Moreover, defenders of American sovereignty, working through their own organizations, must develop international capabilities like the Left's NGOs if they do not already have them. That will ensure both awareness of what the globalists are up to and provide mechanisms to counter them in the often obscure corridors of international organizations, conferences, and negotiations.

Second, we must make foreign policy, national security, and sovereignty issues top priority in evaluating candidates at the federal level, starting with the president. Even at a time of grave economic challenge, we must remember that our international adversaries are not waiting for us to get our domestic house in order. Neither are those seeking to diminish our sovereignty. Indeed, they very well understand the admonition, "Never let a good crisis go to waste." In congressional and presidential elections, we should insist that candidates explain their views on sovereignty, and, if they are incumbents, what they have done to protect it during their terms in office.

Third, we have to ensure that our senators and representatives are reminded regularly that sovereignty issues are important to us. Their attention at election time will be easier to get if they are constantly aware while in office that their constituents think these issues are important.

All of this implies that the importance of threats to American sovereignty needs more

> *Even at a time of grave economic challenge, we must remember that our international adversaries are not waiting for us to get our domestic house in order.*

attention from our political leaders and our media. But most important of all, it needs more attention from us, the citizenry. After all, it's our sovereignty that's at stake. If we don't take it seriously, no one else will.

Copyright © 2010 by John R. Bolton

First American edition published in 2010 by Encounter Books,
an activity of Encounter for Culture and Education, Inc.,
a nonprofit, tax exempt corporation.
Encounter Books website address: www.encounterbooks.com

Manufactured in the United States and printed on
acid-free paper. The paper used in this publication meets
the minimum requirements of ANSI/NISO z39.48–1992
(R 1997) (*Permanence of Paper*).

LIBRARY OF CONGRESS CATALOGING-IN-PUBLICATION DATA

Bolton, John R.
How Barack Obama is endangering our national sovereignty /
by John R. Bolton.
p.   cm. — (Encounter broadsides)
ISBN-13: 978-1-59403-491-6 (pbk. : alk. paper)
ISBN-10: 1-59403-491-5 (pbk. : alk. paper)
1. United States—Foreign relations—2009– 2. Obama, Barack. 3.
Sovereignty. 4. International obligations. I. Title.
JZ1480.B63 2010
320.1′50973—dc22
2010012394

10 9 8 7 6 5 4 3 2 1